CAST OF CHARACTERS

Tammy - (Mom, Auntie)

Robert- (Tammy's present husband)

Granny Gean-(Grandmother)

Sekani- (baby boy)

Antwone- (biological father)

Sylvester- (stepdad)

Kate- (Daughter)

Romeo- (kids' father)

Sheila- (Romeo Mom)

Keyia- (close relative)

DEDICATION

This book is dedicated to all the women who have endured a life journey of traumatic experience who seem to have lost hope and feels as if they can't find the strength to keep moving forward in life. If you are still alive and breathing, God has a purpose and a plan. May you find the courage & strength to know that you are enough, you are worthy, you are strong, and You are loved. Always know that You are never alone. If I overcame my struggles, you could overcome mountains too.

ACKNOWLEDGEMENT

I'm thankful for many things, but mostly GOD...Without him I wouldn't have the strength, the mind, the wisdom, the knowledge, or the health that I must share my story. I am forever thankful for my children who always love me unconditionally and stick by my side. Without them, I don't know where I'd be or what I would be doing. I am thankful for everyone who has been supportive since I began writing my Silence breaker story. If you have made a positive impact on my life since I started my healing journey, just know I am forever thankful, and you are loved.

My prayer is the sharing of my story will help someone to heal, to grant them wisdom of discernment, and to know that they are never alone. Always fight through your struggles and never give up. No matter how weary the road may seem. If you have found yourself in a similar situation to what I have spoken about in sharing my trauma, I encourage you to pray daily, and have faith. When you have found the courage to walk away from anything that no longer serves your purpose, never look back. God sees and knows everything you're going through and have so much instore for you. He´s testing you to see if you're truly ready for the next level that he has planned for your life. When you pray and ask God to change certain things in your life for the better, always believe that he hears your cry. I can assure you that change is not always easy and will not happen overnight, but if you honestly believe in your heart and confess with your mouth, God can turn any situation into miracle at any given time. Perhaps I am living proof that you can go through a great deal of darkness yet become something so beautiful.

Have you ever sat and thought about your life and why things seem to happen the way they do, rather it be good or bad? Sometimes unfair? I'm sure we all have done this at some point in our lives, but as we get older, we realize that everything always happens for a reason. As I reflect on sharing my past trauma of my first book Silence breaker, I realize how blessed I am. The fact that I was born to my biological mother Sherry who died from aids. This is why we were tested from a little infant until the age of 14 to be in such great health is beyond a blessing. This is when I discovered God had a purpose and plan for my life. I survived and can truly say that my life is a blessing and always will be. As I've begun to transition into change, growth and overcoming different seasons in my life that were meant to destroy my destiny. I acknowledged that using my voice and sharing my childhood trauma was a step to breaking a generational curse in my family. Often when our parents endure childhood abuse, they don't have the courage to speak out and use their voice. Instead, they choose to sweep the childhood abuse under the rug, and it becomes a heavy burden they never heal from. Most of the time, this is how generational curses become a domino effect on raising the next generation. In this case, using my voice to share my past trauma was a way to start my healing process and to release a lot of weight that I would carry for so many years. It was time to release myself as a prisoner of my past. Now, as I begin to gain the courage of sharing my silence breaker story, folks would look at my story as a negative impact. They would call my story bashing folks or throwing people under the rug but what they didn't understand was I was walking into a season of exposing several types of abuse that was not normal even when it came to family members. They would view my trauma as a negative insult against me thinking that I would shut down and not want to continue to share my story. I also discovered through each season in my silence breaker story there were signs of physical, verbal, and sexual abuse throughout my life that was also toxic patterns that were not normal. Each chapter in the previous silence breaker story taught me lessons and I gained a lot of knowledge reminding myself that it is not ok to be abused or disrespected in any type of way. Whether it be physical, or verbal abuse. I matter and my feelings did as well. This season in my life taught me how to walk away from anything or anyone that did not value my worth. It taught me true strength and to know that its ok to say "No" whenever I am uncomfortable or not too sure about any situation. It taught me how to put myself first and always listen to my intuition. It also taught me to set boundaries to protect my peace and to always know that it's ok to walk away from anything or anyone who does not value me. Even with my children being involved, it taught me how to put their wellbeing first and to protect them. At the end of the day, I realized that I am their mother, and a mother is supposed to always protect her children. Previously, as I shared my past trauma, I can truly say that all the trials and tribulations made a positive impact on my present life and have changed me for the better. My past has even made me a better woman. Unpredictably, life happens and will continue every day that I am blessed to open my eyes. What's important is that no matter what curve balls life has thrown at me I have survived all my trauma and overcame each obstacle. With each experience that I have encountered in life it has either been a blessing for me or a lesson and I have not one regret of my past.

Chapter 1

BETRAYAL

In 2019, As my childhood trauma would continue to bring a toll on my mind, I finally built up the strength to share my trauma with my mom Tammy. It was time to release the burden that weighed on me for so many years. I called her over and as we sit in my living room area, I'm searching for the words to express my pain while I'm pregnant with my son Sekani. I began to share with her what my stepfather Sylvester (who was her ex-husband) had done to me. The look on Tammy face was terrifying. All she could do was question me. What? When? Where? And how? How could she have been so blind? As tears rolled down her cheeks, she replied: "I knew I hated him for a reason"!! I should have killed his ass a long time ago. She couldn't believe that this was the same man she was once married to for so many years that she thought she could trust and had betrayed her in so many ways. But that crazy part about this was she was already seeing the red flags in Sylvester before she even married him. Tammy sobbing and constantly weeping apologizing numerous times. I replied "I forgive you" Had I not forgiven you, I wouldn't have been able to share my silence with you. We grasped each other very tightly and at that moment, I felt Free! We sat and talked a little more about my trauma as well as a few traumatic issues my mom Tammy endured. Thats when I recognized this was all a generational pattern. Our stories were quite similar. As the clouds got dark the streetlights came on, Tammy apologized one last time and kissed me goodbye as if she was very Sincere about it. Now the crazy part about this is, I thought we both made amends, but obviously Tammy amends meant nothing to her. Once she found out that I would be writing my first book and sharing my survival story with the world, she began to show a different side of her. After Tammy knew that I would be writing my first book she was very unhappy and angry especially after she found out the personal things that I would share in my story. She even started telling her friends and family how the book was not true and how everything I would share was a lie. This is when I really started to see another side of her. This is also when we stopped communicating with each other And had not spoken to each other several months after this. Even with her husband Robert. Her 7th husband to be exact, whom I never liked since the first day Tammy introduced him to me. I had known him from the past at the church home I grew up in and always heard negative things about him that were always true, So I honestly didn't feel like he deserved to even have Tammy as a wife. Years after Tammy and Robert got married, I sensed that there was always a reason why I didn't like Robert ass!

Now let me just say this, it's funny how life works, and we don't always understand the time frame when things happen or why they happen the way they do, but everything is always for a reason and can be blessings. No matter how it made anyone else feel I did what I had to do to feel free. This was also a season I was entering in as exposing things that needed to be shared and not swept under the rug. In this case, I can honestly say that I was glad to share part of my trauma with my mom after so many years, because 2 years later, here comes some devasting news. Everything was so much like a dominant effect one thing happening after another. And just like the seasons, family begin to change, expose themselves, and betrayal was in full effect.

Chapter 2

Exposing Truths

April 11, 2021, my grandma Gean passed away due to massive strokes and suffering from a mental disorder. As I can recall, Grandma Gean was absent most of my life, but it was like the love I had for her was always there. I was her favorite grandchild, and she was my granny. No matter how much hell she would give the family, my love for granny Gean never changed.

Now around the time of my grandmother Geans death I also found out something very devious that happened with a close relative.

March 2021, I go down to the Ocala DMV to purchase a new tag for a new vehicle that I had just bought. While at the Ocala DMV, I found out some fishy but interesting fraudulent activity that I would have never even known about if I had never purchased a new vehicle. As I approached the clerk's service desk, I told the clerk what I was there for. The service clerk never once told me that I could not purchase a new tag for my vehicle but insisted that I had to pay for the tag and sticker that I had on a previous vehicle that was already in my name (that I totally never knew anything about). The only vehicles that I was aware of that I had in my name already were a 2006 kia Sorento SUV and the 2005 Toyota Camry that I just had purchased that same day that I went down to the DMV to have registered to my name. I told the clerk that there must have been some type of mistake, that I should have only had one vehicle in my name at the moment that I was adding the second vehicle which was the 2005 Toyota Camry. This is also when I found out that the vehicle that my cousin Keyia had in my name was a 2008 Toyota Camry. At this point something didn't seem right, and I had a feeling something was off. (All I can say is God works in mysterious ways.) The clerk looked at me as if she didn't believe anything that I was addressing to her, and there I was standing there looking puzzled. I could tell she didn't believe what I was saying because she insisted that if I no longer had another vehicle in my name, that I needed to go down to the Ocala Police Department to file a fraudulent report. I went down to OPD, spoke with a deputy by the name of Officer Sanchez and filed a report. A few weeks after the officer did some deep investigation, He reached out to me about questioning to see if I knew anyone that could have stolen my identity and put a whole car in my name. I told Officer Sanchez I had the slightest clue and could not think of anyone who would do such a thing.

Officer Sanchez: Well, we dug deep into this investigation and have quite a large amount of information for you. Do you know anyone who has a similar address that lives close to you who could have possibly stolen your identity?

Me: Not at all (as I think hard) Feeling deeply confused.

Officer Sanchez: Do you know anyone by the name of Keyia Gordan?

Me: Shockingly!! Yes! Thats a close relative of mine who lives about 2 blocks away from me. I will be seeing her in a few days for a close relative homegoing service.

Officer Sanchez: I know this is a very difficult situation at such a tough time, but it's very important that you keep all information confidential until this investigation is fully resolved.

Me: I will make sure everything is kept confidential until further notice. Thank you, Officer Sanchez, for your hard work and dedication. Enjoy the rest of your day!

Officer Sanchez: Likewise, Ms. Ruth. Talk to you soon.

We hung up the phone. I was more shocked than anything. Like how could someone that I grew up with betray me like this? How much longer did she think it would take for me to find something like this out? I didn't understand why my own relative would do such a thing like this, but I knew it was wrong and one way or another she had to deal with the consequences. I took recognition and pressed charges against her to protect myself and children's wellbeing. I knew it was the right thing to do, and I was at my breaking point in life letting family and people walk all over me. When my family found out that I pressed charges they tried to manipulate me into thinking that I was wrong for pressing charges against her. But I didn't care about their bullshit shenanigans, it was me and my children's life first.

("WHATS DONE IN THE DARK WILL ALWAYS COME TO THE LIGHT").

April 18,2021, the day of my Grandmother Gean homegoing service was held. Of course, I had all these mixed emotions. Knowingly, I was about to face someone that was very close to me who betray me, not only was I dealing with this situation silently but grieving from the death of my grandmother. As the family gathered to start the line up for the service, here comes my cousin Keyia approaching me in a Foney manner. I couldn't believe that she had the audacity to approach me as if she had done nothing wrong and everything was all good. (Well at least she thought everything was all good) because she was not aware that I found out what she had done behind my back. It took so much inside of me to keep everything confidential. Once the investigation was fully resolved, it was no longer confidential. I had the right to share it with anyone and of course with someone that I thought I could possibly trust. I called my mom Tammy and shared with her what my cousin Keyia had done. Tammy was shocked! And could not believe what she was hearing until she seen that I had the paperwork showing proof. She agreed that the whole situation was wrong and during the situation admitted that I needed to do something about it. I felt like there was something I needed to do as well and that was make Keyia be held accountable for her actions. I told my mom Tammy that I would be pressing charges against her and that the vehicle that Keyia put in my name without my consent, would be sold. So, guess what I did? SOLD THE CAR!! Hell, I didn't want the car, but she was sure as hell wasn't keeping it. Now the only person who knew about me taking charge and selling the vehicle was my mom Tammy, she was the only person who I had told. When Tammy found out that I sold the vehicle she asked if she could have $1,400 so that she could move into her new home. And there I was thinking to myself "Damn I done slipped up and told the wrong person I sold that car and got money for it" because as soon as I told my mom Tammy "No" she got upset contacted majority of the family and told the family everything! Again, I felt betrayed not only betrayed, I felt disrespected by Keyia. So, I pressed charges!

Damn! It is your own damn family that will cross you!

Chapter 3

DEVASTATING FOUNDATIONS

September 13, 2021, I get a phone call from Tammy´s best friend from New York City. She tells me that my mom Tammy has passed away from a respiratory infection called covid with pneumonia. Feeling like a bullet piercing my soul, screaming and shouting no!!! Things weren't supposed to be like this! I begin to feel numb after several days of hearing the tragic news of my mom passing. I couldn't believe how everything had happened so fast. I even called up my dad Antwone to share with him the bad news I received and all the mf´er had to say was ¨I'm sorry to hear that, maybe we can now go on with our life¨ I couldn't believe what I was hearing. I felt like I should have had better support from him than just the words of nonsense. People, and even family turned against me, they even thought I'd fall into a guilt trip and enter a vulnerable stage in my life, but little did they know, this situation made me open my eyes. My vision became clearer with life, and I became much wiser. The craziest part about this situation was my own family didn't even reach out to me to let me know my mother had passed and neither did her husband Robert. Again, my mom's best friend in New York City called me up. Someone in a whole other state. There I was once again being betrayed by my own damn family! Several days after the passing of Tammy, a few of my family members reached out to me accusing me of her death saying ¨How me writing my book killed her¨ and another claimed that "Her and I not communicating before she passed killed her". I knew for a fact that I was not the reason my mom Tammy had passed, they just tried to manipulate me into feeling guilty about releasing my book. No type of accountability from my family. There was no way in hell I was letting them guilt trip me into feeling bad about something that needed to be unsilenced and shared. As days went by of my family preparing for the day to lay my mom Tammy to rest, I stumbled across some more disappointing news. Here it was the day I finally discovered why I never really liked Robert deceiving cheating ass! This bastard had the nerve to tell our family that my sister Lisa and I were not welcomed or allowed to my Moma's homegoing service. What type of shit was this? The crazy part about this was the family sat back and let Robert do this and make these types of decisions even when they knew Tammy wouldn't have wanted things to be this way. I felt like it was trying to hurt me more than I had been hurt in the past. Without a fight or a feud, I respected Robert wishes, because there was nobody or anything else that I would let break me again!

In this season in my life God knew exactly what it was that I needed, and what it was that I wanted. I felt like everything that was happening during this process was all a test. It was time for healing and change in my life and for me to be set free from a lot of things. The devil even tried to make me loose hope, he tried to make me lose faith, he even tried to play with my mind and tried to make me question God about everything that was happening in my life, but I was very aware that things were happening for a reason and were necessary. Most of all some things were blessings. I knew that everything that I had ever survived and that I was going through God had not brought me this far for no reason. God had a purpose and a plan for my life. Even through the process of my trials and tribulations God was showing me exactly who was for me and who was not. God even showed me that sometimes walking away from any situation that's meant to destroy you is the best revenge. No matter how hard it may seem.

This was also a season where God was testing my faith on vulnerability. In the process of grieving during Tammy's death Romeo had the audacity to bring his ass around me fake caring with foolish sympathy. I knew deep down that he did not really care that I had lost my mom. All he cared about was the fact that my mom was finally gone and that was just away for him to think that he could slide his ass right back into me and my children's life. Little did he know I was fed up and officially at my breaking point with his ass. He really thought that me losing my second mom would reel me into getting back with him, but he had another thing coming because I didn't care what life throw my way going back to him would never be an option for me again!

2021 was also *the year I discovered I needed to seek grief canceling.*

Chapter 4

SPIRITUAL ABUSE

During the year of 2021, After the passing of my mom Tammy, I felt so confused and lost. I didn't understand why God had taken her from me, so I decided to seek clarity going to the church. The thing that we are taught by our parents is to always seek healing within the church, and when bad things happen to go to church, but that was the wrong thing I did. Running to the church thinking that they would comfort me and pray healing into my life. Instead, they preyed on my life. The crazy part about this situation was one of the members in the church read my book, so they knew my past weakness, most of my traumas and tried to exploit them. They also tried to use my past insecurities against me. The ones that claim to be Christians, right? But instead, it was these church folks that were full of evil spirits. Manipulators, Gas lighters, brainwashers. This is when I discovered that the only person that could fix all my problems and wombs was GOD! This was an episode in my life called "Church hurt" also known as spiritual abuse. This was not the first time that I've gone through this, or even experienced this type of abuse from a church, but I can bet you it will be the last.

Spiritual abuse: is sometimes called religious abuse. It happens when someone uses spiritual or religious beliefs to hurt, scare or to control you.

Chapter 5

A Second Diagnosis

March 8, 2022, my son Sekani was evaluated for Autism. There I was again being a single mother and battling with trying to accept another child that has special needs. And still not one supportive family member and neither was Romeo or his mother Sheila there to show support for our son Sekani. Hell, if they weren't trying to be supportive or helpful in a sincere way, I didn't want they ass around because all they would do is bring more stress to me and more problems and create chaos that my children didn't need to be around. I didn't really expect Romeo ass to be supportive because the whole 8 years we were together he was never supportive in any type of way, and I could never depend on him to be a responsible parent when it came to our children. Even though I didn't have much of a support system at the time, the best part about this situation was I had already known where to get the help and resources that Sekani needed due to me having to go through this process before with my oldest son Kalab when I first found out about his diagnosis. Though I was feeling very alone, and my emotions would linger, I had to pick myself up and remind myself that God had me all the other times and he will continue to have my back and get me through this tough time. This was just another obstacle the devil thought would keep bonded with unhealthy relationships. I knew exactly what I had to do and what needed to be done. And that was to stay away from anything or anyone who was not adding any value or a healthy lifestyle for me or my Childrens wellbeing. Having three children and two of them having specials needs was enough on my plate.

November 8,2022. The day I was discharged from grieving counseling. This is what helped me navigate and cope through the loss of losing my mom Tammy.

New Beginnings

January 24,2022. First day of cosmetology school. During this season of my life, I'm trying another career and outweighing my options to find my purpose. This was another obstacle I struggled with trying to accomplish because of lack of support, But I didn't let lack of support stop me from accomplishing this goal.

March 28,2022 God placed a special person in my life. Not only in my life but my Childrens life as well. This was the first moment in my life that I can honestly say that I experienced real love. And I know you're thinking, "well what if things don't work out with this relationship? Well, it was something different, and felt differernt and for the first time in my life I could say at least I got the chance to experience real love in a relationship, travel the world & shared breath-taking memories, and came across someone who has had my back since they day we´ve first met. This was rare for me, and for this I will forever be thankful to have this experience. In addition to this, all I ever wanted was to be loved, valued, appreciated and to be happy. I had all this right in front of my eyes. This person was also the support that I gained in the process of struggling to finish cosmetology school. With the support of my children and encouraging me to stay focused. With a few of the blessings that I've always asked God for, the enemy tried to step in once again and steal my joy because a few months during cosmetology school Romeo ass still insisted that he could try to show up whenever he felt like he could and try ruin my life again. He would do pop ups to my home unexpectedly and cause chaos and drama with my significant other. Once he realized that him trying to cause unnecessary drama between her and I relationship was not working, He then would try to reach out to our daughter Kate personally and manipulate her into unsafe behaviors. One of the manipulative situations he would try to train Kate was telling her not to tell me and my significant other that he would be stopping by our home unexpectedly. This was a dangerous game he was trying to play, and Kate was not aware of the shit he was trying to pull. All Kate really knew was to do what her dad told her to do. When he realized that his manipulative behavior was not working to get what he wanted, he then started sending verbal threats to my significant. This is when me and my significant other established getting the law involved. Police reports were being made and we were at our wits end with Romeo ass! I felt like he didn't even want me, he just didn't want to see me being happy and moving on to someone else. If he knew someone else was in the picture and had taken his spot, he was always sending threats and harassments. After all the drama, and chaos in my life I made a decision to relocate after I finished cosmetology school. I needed a new start and my children needed to be in a healthier environment.

December 14, 2022. Graduation day! A bittersweet moment. Though I didn't have the support from the ones that I thought should have been there to watch me walk across the stage, there were a few close friends and a few folks that weren't blood related who came to support my success. And for that I was grateful. This was also a fun experience to see if this was also a career that I wanted to pursue. Afterall, I discovered it was not the career or purpose God had instore for me. God had better plans, bigger than I ever imagined. He was just waiting on me to make a move that I had been longing for. A move that I should have made many years ago, but I would let fear get in the way every time.

August 31,2023. I, my children and the special person that I met during the process of me completing cosmetology school relocated to the state of Georgia! A major move. This was my season of stepping out on faith and trusting the process with my life in God's hands. We stayed in a hotel for about 2 ½ months. While living in this hotel God was also opening doors for me that I knew nothing about that totally blew my mind. Being accepted to pursue modeling as a career was a major blessing. A dream that I would always sit as a little girl and tell my mom Tammy that I would pursue one day.

By November 16,2023 we were in our beautiful 2 story home. It felt so peaceful to be in a new environment in our new home.

In 2024, my modeling career took place! Look

Reflections

Growing up throughout my life I never understood why God chose me to endure so much as a child, as a teenager, and as a mother. It wasn't until I became an adult that I discovered that everything that happened to me was necessary. All the obstacles that I ever faced was to teach me, to mold me, and to shape me into the women I have become today. With Life being hard and unpredictable, it's funny how you go through some painful situations just to find your purpose and to see how strong God has built you to be. Nevertheless, God knew that I was built to overcome any obstacle that was brought my way. If he did not think that we couldn't survive it, then he wouldn't bring obstacles to us. We just have to believe in ourselves, keep faith, and never give up. I am always thankful for The Good, Bad and the Ugly for these opened my eyes to see the things that I was not paying attention to before.

About The Author

Through years of verbal, physical, and sexual abuse ranging from childhood through her adult life. She is blessed to say she survived. Battling domestic violence and being molested at a young age. She survived. Despite a few bad decisions she has made in life. She survived. Today she is now living in the state of Georgia. She is currently in the process of Pursuing her new career as a model in Atlanta. She is the voice to inspire all women that their trauma does not have to be a life sentence.

www.ingramcontent.com/pod-product-compliance
Lightning Source LLC
Chambersburg PA
CBHW070109100426
42743CB00012B/2700